T0116905

FREE
FROM
SILENCE

Ronavia Williams

WestBow
PRESS
A DIVISION OF THOMAS NELSON

ISBN: 978-1-4497-1689-9 (sc)
ISBN: 978-1-4497-1690-5 (e)

Library of Congress Control Number: 2011930023

WestBow Press books may be ordered through booksellers or by contacting:

WestBow Press
A Division of Thomas Nelson
1663 Liberty Drive
Bloomington, IN 47403
www.westbowpress.com
1-(866) 928-1240

Printed in the United States of America

WestBow Press rev. date: 07/16/12

Free From Silence

Free- Not Imprisoned or enslaved; not controlled by the obligation or will of another.

From- Used to indicate a specific place or time as a starting point.

Silence- Refusal or failure to speak out. A period of time without speech or noise; Condition or quality of being or keeping still and silent.

NO LONGER LIVING IN CAPTIVITY!
GRATEFULLY, FREE AND MORE ABUNDANTLY THROUGH JESUS CHRIST.

Contents

OUT-POURING POEMS

PRAYER'S AND HYMNS

DOMINATE MISSION

FINAL ANNOTATIONS

Dedication

To the Lord our God, I dedicate this book to you. "*Free from Silence*" is for the glory of your precious son Jesus Christ. Father, you have been my rock when I was without sound. My prayers were never in vain, you have always made your presence known in my life. In this, I have become humbled and now standing on your everlasting promises. Father, you have never left me, nor forsaken me in this journey. Unto this, I thank you.

For a portion of my life, I sought and searched how to please man. My priorities were scrambled and out of order. With gratitude and thanksgiving Father, I thank you for not giving up on me. In your divine nature you have always looked at who you called me to be! Spite my failure to understand your decrees in the past, you loved me. I love you Father and I take this time to dedicate "*Free from Silence*" to you, for your power and your glory. This is only the beginning of so many great things that you have purposed in my life! Therefore, I promise to do "*YOUR WILL*" not man's nor mine. With honor, I will lead your children to you; that they too will do what you have purposed them to do.

Acknowledgements

I acknowledge you Father as first in my life. My cup is overflowing with your grace. Father your comfort, love and discipline have made it possible so that I can rejoice and praise you in spite of my sufferings in life. Being born into death was one thing, being spiritually dead and not acknowledging it because of religious acts was another thing. Thank you for delivering me Father. Without knowing you! I was ready to give up long ago, even take the life you gave me. Father you loved me; your precious fire has and continues to consume me oh, Thank You Abba.

I will like to acknowledge this; The Lord and through trial, error and longsuffering I have learned everything I need is in Christ Jesus. Being a follower of Jesus Christ I have learned how to be obedient to my Father. This obedience has come from the love that I have for my Father, which gives me the desire to do what He says do. Following Jesus has taught me how to trust God and look to Him for "**ALL**" things. Despite **EVERY** situation and **EVERY** circumstance **I TRUST MY ABBA**! Following Jesus, I have learned how to endure longsuffering and how to look towards the hills where there is hope and strength. For I Trust and completely depend on God. With Honor, I acknowledge the Lord our God, my Father being at the forefront of my life.

Breaking Silence

The title "*Free from Silence*" was originally influenced by the thought of me no longer living in a state of silence, and my life in a corner. Breaking the chains of silence and ripping the muzzle off my mouth! I knew it was time to take a stand for God's Kingdom as an ambassador. Sent and commissioned by the Lord Jesus Christ fear has no place to live and doubt has no place to rest its head.

Willingly, I am the vessel that God has and continues to use. With an outward expression I have spent a course of three years; pouring out the words that my Father has poured into me. Apprehensively, satan knows his doom is near and I'm here to proclaim the Good News of Jesus Christ. There are leaders who are leading God's people astray and not representing the Kingdom of Heaven. More than a few church leaders has set up earthly thrones and currently distorting the Word of God.

God Will is that no man parish but, comes to him in repentance. For **godly** grief produces a **repentance** that leads to salvation without regret, whereas worldly grief produces death (2 Corinthians 7:10 **ESV**). Repentance causes you to turn from that which causes you to sin. As a result, your mind is renewed; your heart is changed and prepared for the teachings of Jesus Christ. God wants to give us Eternal Life by accepting Jesus Christ. God is Breaking His Silence to this generation who loves living in sin. Who has no regard to the relationship that God desires with his children. Our heavenly Father is expressing his Love through rebuking, disciplining and correcting this generation who has turned a deaf ear to his truth. For our Father is Holy and Divine He does not co-exist with sin. We were made in his image he desires us to live a life that reflects who he is and his divine nature.

Realistically speaking, take a minute to think about when you were a child. Think about the times when you misbehaved knowing your parents have taught you better! At this time your behavior immediately reflects on your parents.

Therefore, we must not abide in sin and lead a life other than the way God has purposed for us. Beautifully, we were created in God's image to represent who he is. Sin does not align with who God is. Yet, sin aligns with satan who rebelled against God to oppose God's original intent for man. In this, the Lord sent his son Jesus Christ to show us the way into the Kingdom of Heaven. The question is do you desire to enter?

A Note to Readers

False Teachers...

The Lord knows all about your heresies and the whitewash that you use to cover up all your stains. God see's your heart and your motives to confuse his people. You spend your time preaching prosperity gospels that are deep depths and shallow ends. Our Father wrath is burning against you, you simply know the truth and you purposely point His people to you and not the Cross of Salvation. You false teachers make it as though Christ Jesus is not all one needs to sustain them in the faith of Jesus Christ. Woe to you, Woe to you, Woe to you for whom the darkest dungeons await. You close the door in the face of those who try to enter the Kingdom of Heaven and you yourself do not enter... You travel to and foe seeking to win one convert and you make him twice the demon you are.

You rob my people of their purpose; you tie heavy loads on them that you yourself are not willing to lift a finger to carry. For you have burdened my people tying them to titles and committing them to positions that has blinded them along the way. I have turned away from you long ago. You perform a load of religious acts that means nothing to me, your works are in vain and on the Day of Judgment I will tell you to turn from me you worker of iniquity for I never knew you. Less you turn from your sins with a heart of repentance. He, who has an ear, let him hear what the Spirit of the Lord is saying.

God's Lost Sheep...

God loves you so much, he knows all about your struggles, trials and tribulations he is hurting at how far you have drawn from him. God is calling you back home to him; he desires a relationship with you. You have been weighed down so deeply by the things of this world. In fact, you desire the things of this world and the desires of your corrupt flesh more than you desire the heavenly things, eternal things! Stop trying to please man. Look to the Lord; acknowledge Him in all your ways.

When was the last time that you did a review on your lifestyle? When was the last time you examined the things you pursue on a daily basis? Reflecting on this can you honestly say that you love God and he is at the forefront of your life? Or do you live your life according to; I am a good person God knows my heart… I pray, go to church, and pay my tithes and that will get me in heaven! The Bible tell us in **(Matthew 7:13-14 ESV)** "Enter by the narrow gate. For the gate is wide and the way is easy that leads to destruction, and those who enter by it are many. For the gate is narrow and the way is hard that leads to life, and those who find it are few. Are you one of those few? Are you living a life that's pleasing to God's eyesight?

God sits on His glorious throne and love you as dearly loved children; He hates the sin that you pursue. Abidingly, you're so precious to God; he created you with a purpose and a plan in mind! Consider the lifestyle that you pursue! The lifestyle that you're carrying out hinders the relationship that the Father desires with you. Because you have chosen the world over God he has given you over to a deprive mind. **(Romans 1:28 ESV)**

Examine your life! What has caused you to fall away from God? What are you doing that keeps you away from our Father? What's priority in your life? Drinking, Smoking, Sexual immorality, Instant gratification, lust, greed and clubbing! These very things keep you empty and only bring temporary enjoyment that lead to eternal death spiritually and eventually physically! Sin keeps you separated from God. Jesus want's to introduce you to the eternal things, the things that will fill you up for eternity!

The time is right now! Acknowledge the sin that your feet so anxiously rush to. Reflect on all that you have done to sin against God. Right now, ask the Lord to forgive you. Make up in your mind that now is the time to turn from what causes you to sin. Right now! With all of your heart choose the path that the Lord has laid out for you. The Lord has chosen you before the foundation of the world. Jesus desires to walk with you and you with him. Jesus wants you to learn about his teachings, his ways, and his ministry on earth and be cleansed through baptism and the power of the Holy Spirit. Marriage is a vow, a commitment made in front of God. Become married to the Lord Jesus Christ through the baptism of the Holy Spirit.

Jesus is knocking at the door of your heart; will you let him in or shut him out?

Faithful Servants...

Grace and Peace be with you in abundance from our Savior Jesus Christ and God our Heavenly Father who sits on his glorious throne.

Be encouraged! Dearly loved brothers and sisters in Christ. Fight for the faith and stand firm on the Word of God. Build yourselves up daily in the Love of God and the Peace of our Lord. We are waiting for our Savior arrival and it will not be long. This world has become so darkened. Bulks of those who say they are Christians believe their walking in the Light yet, they are walking in darkness! How unfortunate it is that even the chosen among God's people are falling astray and have become perverted, conforming to the wages of this sinful world.

Faithful beloved brothers and sisters there are many false teachers and perverted gospels among you. These teachers are teaching man how to look to them and not the Lord our Savior and all of his supreme being. They are not teaching God's children how to trust in the Holy Spirit. With firmness, I urge you to study to show yourselves approved and trust solely in God. The Holy Spirit will lead you in all truths; search all things out and treat all prophesies you receive with great caution. I pray that you allow Jesus to be the Good Shepherd over your life, for he is perfect and all things in heaven and on earth are subject to him. Our Lord is the perfect Lamb without sin he is perfect in all his ways. Trust solely in the Holy Spirit and avoid every false teaching! For it's not from God.

Woe to the man that lead anyone of you down such a corrupt path, entrapping you in all forms of religious duties and false gospels. Woe to the man who preaches a prosperity gospel. Jesus was crucified and resurrected on the third day; he conquered death and took to the cross with him the sins of the entire world. Be strong in the Lord, and the power of his might. Put on the full armor of God, and know that I am with you ALWAYS says the Lord.

Freedom Time Now

In the beginning was the word in which
All things were formed. The truth in itself
Was the word in itself established by no
one else, other than the One who is the
creator Who created all creation he is
the One I rep.

He is the One who I turn to the channel
of the Holy Bible and tune in to his
divine steps. The One Who ordered my
steps the Most High God The truth in
itself. The One who I rep.

Established by God laws personified
by Jesus Christ, the Lamb without
blemishes Defect or flaws. Believers are
purified By the Word of God in which is
consistent, The Lord our God in which is
reliable. The Holy Spirit who lead and
guides you.

We who worship, we who magnify, we
Who Honor God we who glorify must
do so in spirit and truth! not confined in
a building or restrained to a chair or pew.

He that worship God do it with all of you,
Outside The four walls behind closed doors,
worship God not Man, who will return to
dust softer than sand.

Who is it that have entered in and
divided you? With a sudden change of
directions? Keeping you, hindering you from
obeying God! The truth. The Lord our God
perfecter of perfections.

You were following continually a desirable
activity, actively suffering Christ humility,
lies have slipped in secretly blinding you
completely from the truth rebellion
describes this enemy, this fool.

You are to know that the Kingdom of
Heaven Awaits, for the Kingdom has
been restored to you for this is your rightful
place. You are to know that you are free
in Christ, you are to know that your walk with
Christ has no price for Christ Paid the
ultimate price, give him your life. Offer
your bodies as a total living sacrifice turn
From what's wrong and do what is right in God
Eyes assure yourself that every move you make
Aligns with what the Word of God holds inside.

Who keeps you from knowing that Christ
is all you need? He is the one who sits at
the right hand of God and intercedes. Who
keeps you from knowing that you have the
power and authority to overcome the
Devil schemes? For you have power to
trample satan under your feet.

For my yoke is easy and my burden is light
you're not confined to titles places or position.
How is this possible that you submit to an

earthly leader if you have not submit to the
ultimate leader?

You have not submitted to Jesus, you have
not given up your life to live life through Christ,
yet you are obedient to man, you are not
following God's command place and set
nothing or no one before me. He is God
thee almighty he comes second to none.

What have you gain to faithfully and
Traditionally go to the earthly building
called church yet when you come out you
are spiritually dead, the Lord your God
gives life more abundantly and for eternity
The only death you should consider is dying to
You, your ways and your thoughts time
to become the image of the Lord our
God, the Truth.

You know not my divine will, you know not
My divine purpose for your life! Say's the
Lord. You're holding on to a one day
dream when I have already given you
the key to eternal life say's the Lord.
Who turned you left? When the path
was right? Come out of bondage

For there is freedom in Christ.

FREEDOM TIME NOW

False Teachers

Explode and Unfold
If we really stand up
The harvest is plentiful but the workers are few
Deceiver Demeanor
Seven Churches
False Teachers
WARNING
Teachers who peddle the Word of God

2 Peter 2:1

But there were also false prophets among the people, just as there will be false teachers among you. They will secretly introduce destructive heresies, even denying the sovereign Lord who bought them—bringing swift destruction on themselves.

2 Timothy 2:14

Keep reminding God's people of these things. Warn them before God against quarreling about words; it is of no value, and only ruins those who listen.

Ezekiel 13:8-9

Therefore this is what the Sovereign LORD says: Because of your false words and lying visions, I am against you, declares the Sovereign LORD. My hand will be against the prophets who see false visions and utter lying divinations.

Explode and Unfold

Explode and unfold as I do what
I was told no breeze no shaking of
The trees but I hear a smooth loud
Wind speaking to me.

Awake my child and listen to me,
Explode and unfold that in which I
entrusted in you.

As you speak the words of your God I
Expect you to do what I ask of you
No concern of feelings only discern for this
Very moment you have learned when
the truth shows up the lies appear for your
God did not give you the spirit of fear.

Be of good courage for I am near, explode
And unfold for these fools have hidden
My truth they know who they are, the
Spirit of God is speaking to you.

No storing up in such a temporary place
For the time will come when it all will
Be erased, heaven and earth shall
Past away. Hold dear to all that the
Lord God says.

There has come a time to break
My silence. A God full of, compassion,
Mercy and grace will show his wrath to a

nation rather night or day break blessed is he
that's awake, blessed is he that's awake.
Blessed is he that's awake who ways
Are holy and patiently waits.

Explode and unfold the truth have
been told. To you false teachers lying
creatures teaching my People the
wrong message, forfeiting their blessings
It's the Lord God your testing for the hour is
At hand.

You will reap what you have sown
The idol gods you worship the true and
Living God you have never known.

Your hearts are filled with a manipulative
Skill to blind my people who are spiritually
ill. You false teachers claim that you are
Real, hereis the arrangement! Repent now,
Repent now! You are worse than the tax
collectors. You make as though Jesus Christ is
a bargain, claiming if you want a miracle
sow a seed completely leaving out Repentance
that all man recognizes their sin that
has been hidden, yet your testing
their giving looking pass their spiritual illness.
You have not the power of healing,
I am coming quickly.

If we really Stand Up

If we really stand up, the enemy will
run out of what he calls luck, very abrupt.
No longer will the minds of the young
believers be corrupt the leaders of
deception would be exposed if we
really stand up. Souls would be saved
instead of deceived unbelievers would
believe in Jesus Christ and not man written
doctrines and false prophesies.

If we really stand up, we will follow Christ
walk. Away from what's wrong and live
Christ like. If we really stand up the world
will hate us, the so called Christians
would degrade us. Because, we believe
in one truth not the idolaters. Jesus came
to save us, from captivity and false witnesses,
an idle life stained with blemishes.

Lies are the distribution of you false
Perpetrators full of wickedness. If we
really stand up we will pray for our enemies,
rebuke division and live in unity. If we really
stand up we will be persecuted for Christ sake
because our walk is real and not even
on the list of being fake. The lies are showing,
and some lifestyles are not lining up,
and you know what? I'm standing up.

Jesus paid the price now it's time to fight,

separating the darkness from the light.
If we really stand up we wouldn't be
vulnerable with the things of God.

We will rightly divide the word of truth,
so when the tempter come our armor is on and
not have the wisdom of a fool, But plead the
blood of Jesus over our Christian walk,
we are real and ready for war, Christ is our savior,
and If I offended your behavior, You can speak
to the Lord God our personal savior.

The Harvest is Plentiful, and the Workers are few

Those false teachers are so eager to win your favor, but their intentions
are not good. They are trying to shut you off from me so that you
will pay attention only to them. (**Galatians 4:17 NLT**)

The Harvest is plentiful and the workers are few.
Instead of pointing my people to ME,
You point them to you. Let's clear the misconception
The lies and the deception that does not mirror
God's reflection yet satan and you false teachers
Misrepsentation of the Kingdom of God.
It does not take money financially what a
Conspiracy you hypocrites see you are
My enemies for you hate what is upright. Your
Path is leads to destruction. The just you treat
Unjust as I leave your city my feet I dust. You beg
And plead for money saying plant a seed if
You want to be blessed, have I not called
My people blessed before the foundation
Of the world? You live in distress and honor
Of man causes you to puff your chest
It's the Lord God you test

The Harvest is plentiful and the workers are few
Instead of pointing my people to ME, you
Point them to you. Deformed and conformed
Unborn in a womb that has yet to torn. Your
Wealth is your gut your success is your mess.
You claim that you are blessed to a
Generation that you fail to confess that
I am far from you my blessings do not
Follow you, my anointing does not rest

Upon you. You lead my people astray
You are not one of the chosen few.
Woe to those who can't see past you.

The Harvest is plentiful and the workers are few
Instead of pointing my people to ME, you
Point them to you. You broad of vipers and
Den of thieves you lay waist as pigeons
Waiting to feed. By no means are you
Interested in souls being saved and
Enhancing the Kingdom of Heaven your
Robbing my people and in your hearts my
Words are not embedded. You went to
Get what you were not sent to be whitewash
Your flaws are evident before me. Your words
Speak death and your hearts are wicked
Before me. Your schemes to devise my
People these man made temples,
Titles, positions and greed cripple my
People divide my people. Yet will I
Accomplish what's set out through you.
My Son is the head of the church the
Embodiment of the church. I know my
People and they know my voice. I'm their
Good Shepherd and they're my flock in their
Hearts I have not depart, and when they
Search for me I am not far.

The Harvest is plentiful and the workers are few
Instead of pointing my people to ME, you
Point them to you. See I have raised up a
Generation that will not follow you for they
Know the fruits that you produce
Is cursed at its roots and in you is no truth
Among the wise you are the fool. See, dooms

Day awaits you…. Like spoiled milk your
Expiration date is overdue your debt. to all
You misled all the itchy ears you fed… I'm
A God who keeps my promises and will do
All that I have said.

The Deceiver Demeanor

I see you, and I know what you're all
About your motives to despise and
your hypocritical shouts.

My Father warned me about you false
Prophets. Sad to say you attempt to use
a true believer for your profit.

Define real and you will learn it's
not you, your ways are fake and
hypocritical and I can see through you.

Those poor people don't have
a clue that you are designed to distort
the truth!

Or maybe they do but still decide
to follow the devil in you. Woe to you.
You have no class where is your armor
and holy garment?

You use paste to manipulate
the truth; my God they are in bondage.

Trapped in your lies deceived by your
cries Lord Open up their eye's before they
go completely blind and their spirit dies,
cut off from you, for not knowing the truth.

You gave us a free will, and we have power
to choose. The Deceiver Demeanor knows
the word it roams the earth waiting to be heard.

13

Seven Churches

Church, who has not tolerate wicked
men and false prophets you have preserved
and endured hardship, yet you have forgotten
the captain of the ship! Now's the time to
get a grip, the focus is not to hate the
ways of wicked and false men. But, carry
out the Lord purpose over your plans.
Be grateful of the Lord above.
Come now, back to your first love.

Church, who suffers Poverty,
You're going to need your faith to
endure to the end when the time
come trust the Holy Spirit within,
Your about to be tested from satan.
Just know that you're in line waiting,
to receive the crown of life. Endure to
the point of death use all that you
have left. Trust in the Lord thy God
with your entire heart stand in readiness
this will be a new start! The crown of
life, hold tight the
Kingdom of God in you will fight.

Church, who live in the camp
where satan has his throne, you
have not renounce your faith in
your very own and you have
remained true. However, this stands
against you. What good is it if only you
know my teachingsand my ways? You have

allowed men to be enticed by the false
teachings and idol sacrifices take this
warning and get it right. Take up your
cross and carry it daily don't allow the
teachings of the false. The unbelievers
still need to be taught. Repent and
accept he that was sent, teach all that
will listen.

Church, these are the words of Him
who hold seven stars in his right hand
and walks among the gold lamp stands.
Indicating six out of seven churches
that have been cut off from some area
of birthing.

Church, with the jezebel spirit! You are
indeed foolish. The blood is on your
hands for all whom you mislead.
Congregation, you are all responsible
for your spiritual walk. Spend more
time with God so that you will
understand, doing this will
deter you from idolizing man.

Church, with the reputation of being
so alive, Your about to die. Wake up to that
which is left, Stop being consumed with
your Reputation. Your deeds are not
complete in the eyes of the Lord,
but the eyes of the world. Is it not
my judgment that matter?
Repent, the time is now.

Church, you are lukewarm
neither cold nor hot, and I'm about
to spit you out of my mouth.
You carry along like you have
it all together you're not moved
by my word but the Furs and
the feathers. You have all the
worldly possessions in
deed you have nothing; you're
spiritually dead and live off the
delusions in your head. You
are wretched and have failed
the test, tested. I have come to
you with clothes to cover your
shameful nakedness. Those
whom I love I rebuke stand
the truth, stop living life according
to you. Be earnest and Repent
Hear I am, turn away
from that which has
caused you to sin.

Church, these are the
words from Him that is holy and true,
I have found faithfulness in you.
You, that holds the key of David.
What I have opened no man can shut,
and what I have closed no man can
open. I know your deeds my faithful
seeds. I have placed before you an
open door that no one can shut.
I know that you have a
little strength yet you have kept
my word and have not denied my name.

I will make those who are the synagogue
of satan, who claim to be true Jews
though they are not, but are liars---
I will make them come and fall down
at your feet and acknowledge
that I have loved you. Being that
you have kept my command to
endure patiently, I will also keep
you from the hour of trial that is
going to come upon the whole
world to test those whom live on
the earth.

I am coming soon declares
the Lord. Hold on to that which you
have so that no one may take your
crown, you have endured even till
now. Him who overcomes I will make
a pillar in the temple of my God. Never
again will he leave it. I will write
on him the name of my God and
the name of the city of my God,
the New Jerusalem, which is coming
down out of heaven from my God;
and I will also write on him my new
name. He, who has an ear, let
him hear what the Spirit of the Lord
Is saying.

False Teachers

See this is what I understand,
says the Son of Man There has been
some teachings according to the
plans of man and not for the very
reason I took my stand.

These fools honor me with their lips but,
their hearts are far from me and
their focus is to look for men
and women to deceive, I tell
you the truth if you don't repent the
fiery abyss is where you will be sent.

Out of my mouth I will spit you says the Lord.
I will not think twice because I am
warning you. Warning comes before
destruction and again this is your
warning repent now and turn away
from your sins.

Are you daft? You worship me
in vain you mean nothing from
your heart, but you call on my name.
The blood is on your hands for each
man you have deceived, and mislead.

I call men to repent and believe
and you false ministers, pastors, and
prophets you confuse them with all
they have to do is sow a seed

And then they will receive prosperity.
Did John the Baptist not preach
repentance? who are you to take my
word and make my truth hidden?

I rebuke and discipline those whom
I love; turn from your wicked and
deceiving desires turn from the false
teaching and preaching which has become
a worldly empire. I the Lord God am not with
You. Your own evil desires has inspired
this! The time is now that your heart is
cleansed. Take this time now
to repent.
My messenger was sent, I the Lord God
can see that you think the Holy Spirit
is dwelling within you, I am far from you.
demon spirits are controlling you.
I rebuke and discipline those whom
I love. Take your eyes off financial
gain and fix them on the things
above. Many times you have
turned your ears from that in which
I said, all to please yourself and
Man! You are so focused on the
Offering tray, you cannot see that
I am the way.

I am the Lord God and have
the power to take it all away;
the building church, the pews
see I'm warning you. You have gotten
beside yourself I can take it all
including the very little you have left. So,
you take this opportunity to repent and
bring to an end operating in the
spirit of Balaam.

WARNING

I tell you now that you are dead and
only through Christ will you be made
alive. On Christ is where you must
fix your eyes.

Fix your eyes on the things above the
world cannot give you the truth, yet a
free trip to lies and deceit and a life
time of being confused.

I tell you the truth I am not there I abide in
unity I see that you rather settle for unbelief
because without hardship you
are pleased.

I tell you now that you are far from
me. Those whom I love I rebuke and
discipline I do not leave you like
lost sheep; I give you the choice to
believe and the opportunity to know.

I use you for my power! And my glory!
that which is eternal you will not have
room enough to receive turn from that
which is temporary and turn to me.

Your sins have sold you a fantasy
that's full of corruption. I the Lord God
is interrupting and giving you a chance.
The choice is yours, and you cannot say

that there were no warnings.

A falling nation will hear my Gospel,
it will be delivered with fire and
when the time is proper. Keep your
eyes open so that you do see the
warnings of the time. I encourage you
to start a new life through Jesus Christ.

Time and time again I have brought this
message that has not changed; in different
ways to you it came. Purify yourself
starting with your hearts.

I know the plans I have for you it's
defiantly not a sin driven life it's
turning from sin and surrendering
to a new Life through Christ.

Only by your repentance will
you receive forgiveness so do not
listen to those who preach my word
saying that you will be set free without
repentance! This is my very intentions that
you acknowledge that which brought you
far from me.

Like a child you will remember that which
is not good and long to that which is
right, I AM He that gives life. I AM
the One who will lift up a standard
when the enemy comes at you
to strike.

Take your sword and trust and believe
that I AM He that foresees, without warning
you will never know. Because, I love you
I have come to let you know
the time is now.

You are about to be cut off from
Me! Your ways of living has
disgusted me.

Teachers who peddle the Word of God

You Balaam Teachers have spread a yeast
among God's people you're ways are
See through false teachers yearn profits
you're covetness are humongous
And out grown.

Your will to help God's people your thrill
Comes from robbing God's people not
at all interested in the souls
Of God's people.

Material increase, pews increase,
Audience Increase offering tray increase,
New automotive increase.

Souls saved decrease, souls delivered
and set free decrease, hunger for the
gospel decrease, speaking the truth,
decrease. Thirst for God's love decreased.

Tell me says the Lord that your
Motives are not plain to see. You have set
yourself up as an idol before men. You have
taught them to look to you and not me
say's the Lord.

You have turned men to depend and
trust on you and not me say's the Lord.
Hypocritically defect Conformed by the
world and dislect you Are satan outlets!
With no necessity to Inspect its Balaam
you reflect. Stubborn as can be.

My truth has been made clear to you! You
have studied yet, not understood the
blood is on your hands for every soul
You misled. Without pity, petition or
request my ways you left! Woe to you
teachers that will experience the
second death.

Temple

Our temple, the temple our centered
place the centered place of worship.
The priority place of where it's established
and begins the source of God plans the
resources will follow then. Our temple the
temple our centered place the centered
place of worship. In God's presence no one is
around there is no congregation just you
and God.

Humble before his throne, seeking His face
asking for Understanding glorifying his
majesty! bring your temple in the presence
of God, your body, soul and mind.
Your Spirit the divine Spirit of God's image.

Who desires to worship? It's not found
in the earthly temples it's found and
derived from the ultimate Established
Temple. Offer your bodies, your minds,
and your hearts to the Living God as
sacrifices! Living sacrifices, of holiness,
pureness, clean without blemishes.

Change the way that you are living,
your mindset has Lack! Who longs to
know where at? Worship God in Spirit and
Truth. The Lord's divine all power all knowing
Wisdom, he poured out His Spirit on all
flesh your body is a temple. We received
the spirit, the image of God.

Reflecting God's holiness, his wholeness his
Divineness. Our Father who art in heaven, His
Spirit his image he has poured out on us.
He that worship must, worship in spirit and in truth.
Living out God's divine principles his word.
We are the established temples, the living epistles,
Taking God's principles to the earthly temples.
Our spiritual act of worship, giving the Lord
Our bodies, our minds, our soul and hearts
From his presence we are not to depart.

For the Lord communicates to our hearts.
Far more than a few of the building called
Churches has become a misrepresentation a
Completely hocus pocus; these so called
leaders have shifted your focus! The Lord's
worship you have not Chosen yet mans will.
You have forsaken God's divine will That
no man be lost, that no man parish. Yet, your
commitment and faithfulness to going to
the building this is what you cherish you have
no relationship with the Father yet, this you cherish.

Have you lost and distorted site? It's The Lord
your God you seek with a vow and faithfulness
with all your might! Awake from your sleep and
worship at the throne even in the middle
of the night.

Awaken the temples inside of you! Forsake not
The Lord your God. For I am your first love Put
nothing and no one above, not earthly leaders
No race of people, no objects, you are not

Subjects you are sons of the New Covenant
You are spiritual temples that causes even satan
to tremble. For you are my dearly
loved children, Mypeople that holds
inside of you a spiritual temple.

TEMPLE

Lost Sheep

Today
The Pursuit of Love
Know the Truth
Circumcised
I worship you
I am not measured by my pockets, but I am measured by my faith
We are not our own
We are here on business
Purpose
Jesus means so much more

Jeremiah 50:6
"My people have been lost sheep; their shepherds have led them astray and caused them to roam on the mountains. They wandered over mountain and hill and forgot their own resting place.
Matthew 10:6
Go rather to the lost sheep of Israel.

Today

Today a God who need not to
compromise A God who's longing
that you open up your heart and
eyes that you not be blind trying to
bring him down to your size as if
he's not God alone as if he don't
stand alone he's God by himself and
needs no one else so in deed its time
that you die to yourself you're selfish
ambition keeps you from paying
attention to the love that Our Father
has given us from the beginning the
love that he has not kept hidden pride
keeps you from listening to the voice
that that's too dear to be hidden to
choose the world over God you have
to be kidding.

Today Serve him with your lifestyle not
later yet now For Jesus Christ has shown
us how. Stop being so quick to complain,
jealous envious, rebellious and disobedient
reflecting not God's Image yet satan and
all his wickedness. Where is your zeal to serve
the Lord to take a hold of your calling in the
body of Christ offering your body as a living
sacrifice your being your living you're listening
your time simply acknowledge the Father
in all your ways he's supreme and wants
all of you today.

Today lay down your idols the arrogance
that you have behind your titles that
you went to get and were not sent to be
everything that you place before God is
your god examine your hearts who's desperate
to love the Lord to give him all of you I was
you calling on the Father only when I thought
I need him the most and now he's everything
I need and more focused on the heavenly things
that's in store. Stop listening to prosperity
gospels that tells you all about worldly prosperity
when inside the wisdom of the Lord you lack in
fact to the deep ends shallow and broken for
the Lord wants all of you seek him for restoring.

Desire his glory his presence, get lost in his presence
for Our Father is a King who sends us to represent
His Kingdom to extend the invitation to all who is
experiencing separation and have become lost in
their transgression. And simply I pray desirability
that the desperation to know the Father
overwhelm you take a hold of you to serve love
and desire what our Father desires for you
become not tired contend for the faith for our
Father wants all of you Today.

The Pursuit of Love

As the years fly by and the days walk by,
The hours are lazy the minutes are steady
And the seconds are weary.Bracing the time
Valuing what's prime, I long with desire I will with
Inspire and I hope with my entire heart.

Night breaks and a white dove pass by
The one He love, He chastens. May they be
Attentive to His words and He to their ways.

Love is patient Love is Kind Love
Is always on time. He loved her first,
Even when she did not know. The nations
Described as daughters and cities as sisters.
Love was always there. He loved us first
And to think of the times we deserted love we
Are so undeserving of love yet without stretched
Arms love welcomes us.

How can any living being be placed
Before He that created all things
Giving me a reason in this season
And a chance to reason may my case be
Pleasing because life as I knew it was a
tease and Love has been keeping me.
The times I walked away to experience
temporary things. Even in that time and this
current time Eternal life was and is the dish
dished out and a reward being desert
according to my works.

Love pursued me patiently, willingly
waiting, creatively creating, a life birthed
and purposed For His worshiping and
His praising. Time after time Love pursues
Love is what he do, Love is who He is.
It's not about in the meantime or in
between time see life as I know it is real
time and love works overtime and
this generation is behind time because
Love has been pursuing us since the
beginning of time not wasting time
yet pursuing us time after time.

Love, I submit to you, I embrace
you! I will, to take my time understanding
you. For the times when I don't know I trust you.
I wait patiently upon you, surrendering all to
you. What is a greater gift? Then giving
up all to please you? All to pursue you?
All to be identified in you?

For the greatest gift that you have given
me was your Son! For the Greatest gift that I
attain is salvation and the outpouring of your
love. Identified even in my pain, my comfort,
when I'm dismayed the love that never Fades!
May nothing do us apart.

Love, I promise to Love you, and place nothing
and no one before you. My heart belongs
to you. Everything of who I am seeketh you.
Everything of who I am pursues you! I'm lost
without you there's no breath to breathe no
reason to believe, no hope to say
hopefully for all my days I desire
you close to me.

My shelter, it's your presence that consoles
me! Pursuing Love is my destiny living for love is
where I'm meant to be. Willingly, I desire what
you desire for me.

Your words are trustworthy. Words can
never express actions can never be my
best even my last Breathing breath is
not enough to confess that pursuing you
is all that I have left.

You are the extra miles that I take,
the extra hours that I wait the very
reason I have faith. When everyone
turned their back on me... even when I
gave up on me! You breathe life in me
enabling me to catch my breath and
breathe.

Tossed up and down Lord, You simply took
my frowns and gave me smiles you're not
Worth my while but you is my while.
Lord, you pursued me without a doubt
Therefore, I spend this life pursuing
You "Love" in these miles.

Know the Truth

Jesus sent out all believers to preach
the Gospel Not, to be an eternal
follower of man but an eternal
follower of the God Man Jesus Christ,
our Lord who gives the righteous favor
based on their heart faith and behavior.

Join me in the Kingdom of God
unhardened your hearts surrender to
the Lord pick up your sword. The time is now
to be Kingdom minded the fact of the
matter is ignorance has kept you blinded.

Not knowing the truth, yet attracted to the
worldly things, Got you thinking you're
the next hottest thing! Think again, the only
thing your focused on is making it rain
get this one thing through your brain and
marinate in your spirit. Without holiness you
will not see the Lord. How can you Love
someone you haven't accepted in
your heart?

Yet you got your "boo" tatted all over
you! Brothers and Sisters, get a clue,
the worldly things have consumed you.
I know because I was there too. The
time is now that you know the truth;
Jesus Christ came to save me and you.

Holiness- moral purity, to be set apart
and sanctified for service to God.
Pay attention, no where does it say,
it's okay to compromise the Word of
God. Hoping that God understand
my lies because, I'm so focused on my
life for Him I have no time. After all, He
is life, and gave you life so that you
maybe just like Him.

Ministry use to be a mystery but ever
since I've been walking with Christ in my
heart every minute, hour, and day has
been a new discovery. Ministry-A service
in the name of God. Such service after the
example of Christ all Christians are called to
be ambassadors for Christ.

So turn away from what looks good.
Gain a relationship with God all this religion
is separating us further and further apart.
Consequently, missing out on some small factors
like Love thy Neighbor, even after he or she has
slandered your name.

If the Love of God is in your heart it
will flush out what's vain and allow the truth
to remain. For it is the sinners Christ came
to save.

Circumcised

Circumcised, and made alive through
Christ, not in the state of mind of thinking twice
but, giving up the good life to live right.
Tempted and hard pressed on every side
still will I remain circumcised.Covered by t
he blood and, the Lord is my judge, The
Holy Spirit is the agent of my conviction.
Father examine my heart.

Circumcised, in the New Testament
symbolic to casting off sin or worldly
desires deep within. My heart is fixed
on the things of God. So, I say to satan
and his worldly possessions get ye behind
me stay under my feet, I mean that with a
passion you see.

Circumcised, and made alive through
Christ. I tried my way day after day and I
tell you now nothing compares to where
I am now. Saved sanctified and full baptized
not to mention circumcised!

What a new birthing no worries, emotional
hurting I'm rejoicing! In tough times I refuse
to be distracted from the ultimate purpose.
My eyes are on the prize. My old man was
worthless! God get's his glory for eternity from
me. I am not mans fool my reward is not here
on earth, God can turn your life around too.

There's a much bigger picture so get a bigger
frame, and change you lenses repent now.
Everything about you needs cleansing.

Circumcised, and made alive through Christ
try him for yourself I guarantee he will make
all things right! Giving you understanding of
what should and should not be. Your key is to
surrender to Him completely! Allow Him to be
the number one you seek.

Circumcised, and made alive through Christ,
join me in this mission, this is one trip you don't
need mans permission! Jesus Christ has
already signed the petition. So listen, repent
now and be circumcised through Christ you
will be made alive.

I Worship You

You entered this world unknown to many,
believed by some, and all who stood up for
you were close to none. Your word was written
and brought to life. They who? The Jews, Gentiles,
Romans, it doesn't matter if your black white
green or blue they knew the truth and still
refused to... Accept you.

The good news is I worship you. Only by
your blood I'm able to receive remission.
Only by your love, grace, and mercy
I'm able to experience repentance.
Drawing near to you and you near to me.
My God I thank you for peace. Cleared
of my conscience, made holy and set
apart for you to use... My, my the good
news is I worship you.

A little testimony if I may, I wasn't always
black or white; I had some gray, living
according to me. If anyone asked... "I'm a
Christian Is what I would say".

Exploring the mind of a youth, full time
student of being fooled, saying I'm a
Christian but my ways was not like you.
Only through Christ I'm able to get to God.
Through Christ were stripped of our ways that
we may appear as one holy to God. And his
commands! He want written to our hearts.

The Good News Is I Worship You. I'm calling
out the prostitutes, drug dealers, lying crooks
and criminals, the unbelievers, adulterer's
fornicators, and idolaters the Good news is
Christ came to save us. So, no longer are you
a victim to your sins using your past as an
excuse to why you're failing.

Jesus already paid the price. So that we can
no longer be dead but, exposed to life through
Jesus Christ. The Good News Is We Worship You.

I am not measured by my pockets, but I am measured by my faith.

I am not measured by my pockets but by my
faith, my will to take the light in the darkest place.
Answering to God, when he directs me in my
Path, I say yes father which way? I'm not
measured by my pockets but, I am measured
by my faith. In the Old Testament it was declared
the Lord our God will rebuke the devour
from our crops. But in the New Testament there
was a new covenant and Christ changed my heart.
Don't get it twisted God's word never changes
it remains the same But, when Christ came it
changed the way we do things. Jesus said in this
world we live, there is constant change this is
why he wants the law to be written on our
hearts. He wants us to be born of the spirit and
change how we're living. Because it's not pleasing
to God. And it's only by our faith were able to
move God.

When did we get here? As if it takes
a financial seed to please God? When it's
Obedience, sacrifice, faith and the renewing
of our hearts. Giving up our worldly desires
and all the burning passions we had that only
made us a liar. I'm not measured by my pockets
but I am measured by my faith. Only by my deeds will
I be justified, and ever since I have been following
Christ I'm no longer dead, in fact I feel so
alive.

While I was spiritually healing God
was doing a natural cleansing. Clearing out
all the ungodliness, that wasn't pleasing to
God. In fact, those very things were
disgusting and broke his heart.
God look down on me and seen my
willingness to live according to his
holiness. It didn't take fifty dollars
in fact it didn't take one cent. But, what
it did take was for me to fall to my knees
and say Lord God I repent. Yes to your
will and yes to your way, He said my
child no longer do you have to cry this
battle is not yours and EVERYTHING
will be okay... I'm not measured by my
pockets but, I am measured by my faith.

Now the word of God have manifested
it's not the hears of the word that's declared
righteous in God's sight. It's the doers
of God's word who serve God, with all
their might. I'm not in the group of those
who refuses God's word. I said, I'm no
longer in the group of those,
who hears God's voice and
Refuses. I'm the one who He
willingly uses.

We are called to be ambassadors
so don't get thrown off from titles. Minister
prophet or pastor. I was called to be an
ambassador to preach the Gospel through
spoken word. What have you done? Who
have you saved? Who did you tell, God

will make a way? See I'm not measured by
my pockets but I am measured by my faith.
Without faith, it's impossible to please God.
And the only reason he challenges you to give,
is to see if you will obey, In this case he's testing
your faith. It's not your money God wants it's
your faith.

Living for God will result to giving spiritually,
physically, mentally, and financially. I'm not measured
by my pockets but, I am measured by my faith because
see if that wasn't the case I would be able to
purchase all that I need in order to be saved.

So don't
get it twisted when I say I am not measured by
my pockets but I am measured by my faith. Preaching
the Gospel and baring a testimony of the reason
I even have faith. Again without faith it's
impossible to please God, and his laws... He
want written on our hearts... To have faith,
the power of believing without seeing, the
power of hoping without knowing. Listen
and allow your mind to be re-taught, sorry
for thinking aloud I just can't deny these
thoughts, God use me to speak the truth
in which others fought... And by Christ
resurrection our sins were brought. I'm on
a path of truth the Holy Spirit can't be
misused manipulated and abused so the
lies I refuse so that I can follow the truth.

Observe the daily things you skip on doing, how
you sow five hundred dollars and, you
think you're replenished and ready for using...

please believe it's not God you're fooling.
Did you forget the hint to repent? And turn
from your wicked ways so that your soul
will be saved? It's not your pockets
but it's your faith.

So in life we have the givers and the takers.
Now the givers they give, not just financially but,
Spiritually emotionally, physically, mentally
Naturally. The givers give to God,
by their faith. So hear me when I say. It
was Abraham faith that he was ready to
sacrifice his son. God said wait, you
believed so out of you a nation of believers
will come. So because of his power to stand
up and be a believer I'm a reaper. David
was a man after God's own heart his readiness
and obedience set him apart. Samuel was sown
as a seed to God he was born to live for God,
God called him three times and the fourth time
he said here I am, God had a plan Samuel
carried it out. His faith made him whole.
Living for God he gives you the power
to be bold. Woe to you who are on sleep
mode.

Takers, who take and never give,
is this really how you want to live? God
called you and you turned your ear.... If you
don't fear anything else, it's him you fear.
Open up your hearts and allow Christ Jesus
to give you a fresh start. I am not measured
by my pockets but I am measured
by my faith. So don't measure my pockets,
because I'm studying

God's word, living for him, and there's
no stopping.

See the Holy Spirit is on me
right now and I'm not seeking to gain or
win an earthly crown but, I'm here to preach The
Gospel and turn the thoughts of giving
around. Giving to God will result to giving
to others surrendering to his will and his way,
nothing that was created or man-made. God is
my first priority I'm not living out of a fantasy
but the spiritual reality. What is it that God
called me to do? What is it that God called
you to do? I must proclaim I'm not a fool
but an individual on fire for Christ and hungry
and thirsty for spiritual food. I'm justified by
my works which takes faith every day. And
when God called me I didn't say wait… So
please believe I'm not measured by my pockets
but, I am measured by my faith.

We are not our Own

I die to my flesh daily, the thoughts of Christ
Crucifixion grieves me, and stimulates my spirit.
How dare me to say "I'm living my life".
When Jesus gave up his life that, I may be
Just like him. It pierces my soul and unfolds my
Flesh that out of millions I was Chose.

I am not my own, I died to the flesh so that
Christ can own me. In the inconsistency of
Mankind I'm constantly being grateful
of God's ultimate plan, for me.

I worship God in spirit and in truth. What God
Call grounded, the world calls confused? For the
wisdom of the world has been made foolish The
Holy Spirit is my comforter. He brings consultation,
correction and revelation to the doubters.

I am not my own, yet you attempt to define
who I am, And what I'm not, when God called
me to his purpose so being who you want me
to be I will not.

My voice is softly spoken, my spirit evokes the
truth, I stand humbly with a sound mind saying,
who I am. Better yet who are you?

You are not your own your flesh died so God can
own you. Daily you're trying to figure it out
when the Word of God declares he has

already worked it out. So, break the
ungodly soul ties, which create ungodliness
unrighteousness disobedience and a
life of living lies. Understand God is nothing but
truth. So, stop asking me who I am and
define you.

You are not your own, you died so Christ
can own you. I am not my own and I can
never be cloned, Christ paid our loan he died
for our sins, He came here in the flesh just so we
can have a reason to no longer live like
heathens! But to spend our life believing that
God sent His only begotten Son so that
whoever believe in Him shall not parish
but have eternal life. Christ paid thee
ultimate price and we are not our own.

We are Here on Business

Brothers and sisters, stop tripping!
We are here on business. Just in case
you forgot, sit down and listen! This
temporary place is in desperate need
to be embraced by the godly things!
Throwing out the worldly things and
being replaced.

Believers, take your place, and get
on your post. Prepare the way for our
Heavenly Host. Cut, it, out we came
here to browse. To recognize
the weakness and operate in
meekness. Take back, the Kingdom of
God which was attempted to be
comprised from the very start.

satan, you are a liar, you just
need to embrace your punishment
and burn, burn, burn in the lake
of fire. Our youth will know the truth!
I don't care how big your demons is,
you must not know how big my
God is. Have a seat your knees are
weak and the Holy Spirit is about
to speak.

We are here on Business,
not to operate in the flesh and
deny Christ has risen. I am in prison
locked down in the Word of God
with truth around my waste,
righteousness on my breastplate, and
with a readiness of a shield called faith.
A helmet of salvation, with the sword
of the spirit, my feet
is felted in the ground, wait!
Did you hear that sound?

Holy, Holy, Holy is this ground.
For this you might want to stick
around because the Kingdom of God
is here to turn some lives around.
But don't trip because the
United States is not where I
own my actual citizenship, I'm just
here on a business trip.

We believers are here on a mission, to
declare the Most High dwelling
place. In our hearts the
Kingdom of God so let's run this
race.

Believers, our home
is in the atmosphere where God
dwells so if you're playing church
with make-up of holiness but,
inside your heart there's dirt! You're
in first class mail delivered

straight to hell. The Kingdom of God
and his righteousness will prevail.

Believers, and unbelievers,
I am not limited to just the
Christians, We are Here on
Business, to take back what
the devil stole from us.
I did not come to find your right
spot and rub it, I just might disturb it,
and just in case you haven't heard it,
here's the verdict. The time is now to
repent turn away from your sin so that
the Holy Spirit can dwell within.
Convict and crucify the flesh which is
consumed with worldly mess! And
if you don't turn from your wicked ways like
the material things you will get left.

Excuse me if I touched a nerve
it really doesn't matter when
the Holy Spirit needs to be heard.
Just in case you walk away you
can't say that there was no warning
that your soul needed to be saved.

It doesn't matter what's your
religion, culture, or tradition is there is
one thing that needs not to be hidden,
the Kingdom of God is at hand
and calling all nations to repentance.
The Holy Spirit comes with fire,
conviction and full of truth. Give

your life to Christ and leave the
worldly things behind you.

Don't trip, get a grip. The
United Stated is not where I own my
actual citizenship I'm here on
Business, so if it was you I offended it was
intended because the Holy Spirit
dwells in me with no limits. But don't
trip because the United States is
not where I own my citizenship, I'm just
passing through to declare the
Good News, don't be fooled because the
devil dresses just like you. That's why
it's important that your heart be pure
and true. So join me when I say...
satan, you are a liar you just need to
embrace your punishment and burn,
burn, burn in the lake of fire.

See power belongs to God, it did from the
Very start where there is malice,
idol worship, hatred and gossip you
need to examine your heart especially
if it doesn't line up with God holy laws.

Young women, where is your Holy Garment?
Cover up your body parts because you're
attracting the wrong spirits and God is
not in their hearts. If so they will let you
know that you don't have to be half naked.

Holy, Holy, Holy is the name of the Lamb
that was slain. Don't trip we are here on
Business, to proclaim Jesus name so
pick up your cross and let's go get the lost.
This is a generation that is in desperate need to
Be reconciled back to God.

Purpose

What were you purposed to do? When you're
looking at Life from the worlds view your
purpose may not Interest you.

Yet, draw near to God and he near to you.
We all have a purpose, and Work for the
Kingdom to do.

God will show you what you were purposed
to do. God wants to use you. For His glory, for He
alone is truth.

Purpose, is bigger than our plans it prioritize
our lives no longer living in strife or doing
Idol things with our time.

Purpose, is bigger than our plans step
out on faith and dare to be who some
said you can't. If God be for you who can
be against you? This I can assure you,
Indeed you can get fired from a nine to
Five but not what you were purposed to do!
The Holy Spirit and his angels
are behind you, break the chains,
and bind the generation curses.
The time is now that your purpose is
Birthed.

Join me, as we explore Proverbs
the sixteenth chapter and third verse.
Commit your works unto the Lord

and your purpose shall be established.
Untouchable and lavished.
What do you rather? Live in the world
and conceive corrupt thoughts,
circle your life around material things
and the latest shoes you brought?
That's not Life, that's your flesh taking
a joy ride on the dark side.

Purpose, get in it now, Jesus Christ is our savior
Through him we receive our crown.
The Kingdom of God and its righteousness
Is relevant making all other things irrelevant.
Question? Do you feel like you have gone to
school half of your life and there is
still a void in you? What's given by
man is temporary to the flesh, what God has
for you is an eternal promise that's in place
just for you. Seek him now for that
which you were purposed to do.

Jesus Means So much More

Jesus means so much more than
the day to day things that we live for
and the things that we prioritize
to do these very things has used us
and caused us to look like a fool but,
in the end Father, we miss out on you.
Jesus you mean so much more than
life itself take it away so that the daily
Things we may be stripped of. Our worldly
ways sacrificing on earth thanking God
for the spiritual rebirth... In the end
tell me what will your street life be
worth? Materialistic things worldly
perks... To God this hurts, a nation
choosing the wrong path not realizing
their losing until they have been
stripped to where it hurts being
justified by their works in the end what
will it be worth?

God, you breathed into man made me
from his rib and now I take this breath
to give you all that I have left. Your
presence hasn't left me even when I left
your presence thinking that the world
can give me love and the best presents...
You are the beginning of love you are the one
I put no one above! You mean so much more...
When will each eye open? No, I will take the
time to impart this message in each person...

to all who is willing to listen with
unhardened hearts and who is drained of the
world and ready for the renewing of their
hearts the time is now, Jesus Is the answer
and with him is where you start.

He means so much more than your heartache
and pain and right now you're going insane.
The only way out is drugs, sex, lies and
being behind prison doors to remain sane.
Here's the remedy to your pain. Stop what
you're doing and call on Jesus name. Jesus is
the beginning and the end He is that humble
voice that's speaking within. He is the One
you don't have to fight with till you win he
is the One who understands where you been,
He is the One who knows where you're going,
He is the One with the keys to eternal life He
is the One who heals you by his stripes, He is the
One who listens in the middle of the night…
He is the One who took you from the dark and
placed you in the light. He is the One who placed
your feet on solid ground, he is the One where
you're no longer lost but found. He is the One
that when he is there you don't
need anyone else around….

He means so much more so don't close, but
open that door it was our iniquities he suffered
for. See it was our redemption He bleed for so that
we are reconciled back to God. Be wise and
not foolish and be the vessel that God uses.
Your body, don't abuse it life in hell is eternal
ruin brothers and sisters, think about what
you're doing he means so much more.

This world is a trap;
this walk was not set to be easy
for we rejoice in our sufferings.
For I am the voice of the One greater, who is
disturbed of the spiritual voids, silence your
voice to hear His voice. Be quicken to listen and
slow to speak be your strongest when you're weak
technically Jesus bloods speak.

My Lord, you're so much more then I was destined
for, you're so much more then I was purposed
for. You're so much more then I live for, you're so
much more…. Let the heavens and the earth
proclaim Holy is the Lamb that was slain. Jesus
has risen to bring this world healing.
The time is now that your worldly desires be ended
experience God's forgiveness caused by your
repentance.

Power Demand in the Desert

Oh, living beings, your hearts are hardened
and stubborn. You hear what you want
To hear, you shed tears for everything
And everyone else except, the one you are
To honor with expressed emotions. I am he
That is worthy the one who calls you
Dearly loved children. Your ways, your plans
The life I have given you has become
Centered around you and things. Am I not
he that created you? Poured my spirit on
you? Am I not he that you are to be true
to? Am I not he that is able to save you?

In this life you live there is more than
You know of lack, every window is open
Leaving space, opportunity and room for
satan's attack. The life that you call life
Is uninteresting and unproductive to me
It has no meaning and sin is your best friend.
You have evil and rebellion desires.
For it is only yourself that you are deceiving.

Lean on me, bring your worries, your cares to me.
I am he that is Just, Majesty and Almighty.
Fight off sin declare it renounced as a friend
Tell it that the Lord is your God and does not
Co-exists with the rebellion of sin.
Make willing your heart to seek the
Lord your God, make willing your mindsets
To know the truth. Receive Jesus Christ the One

You're to follow, the One who knows eternal
Life. For I am your God. My will is that you
Not parish or be lost, but have eternal life.

This world is temporary for it
Is a speck of time! One day is like a thousand
Years, and a thousand years is but one day to
The Lord your God. The Time is right now
That you change your mindsets and open your
hearts. Study the teachings of Jesus Christ is
where you start; seek nothing and no one else
Other than the Lord your God.

Power Demand in the Desert

Lost Sheep

The Blood of the Lamb
Lead Me Home
How He Loves Us
Apostasy
Kill, Steal and Destroy
One Life to Live
Influenced by satan
Our Father's Love
Examine Me
No Greater Love
Remnant
Lead Me Home (Re-insert)

Acts 26:18
Open their eyes and turn them from darkness to light and from the power of Satan to God, so that they may receive forgiveness of sins and a place among those who are sanctified by faith in me.

1 John 1:6
If we claim to have fellowship with him and yet walk in the darkness, we lie and do not live out the truth.

The Blood of the Lamb

The Blood of the lamb shed for
our sins, may his grace keep
us out of our transgressions. His power
is mighty his peace is sufficiant his love
shows me owns me consoles me, like no
other he is the almighty. To fail is
not in his plans. Brothers and sisters it's
not likely it's not he.the perfect Lamb without
sin he came in to take out sin. He in us
and we in him there is no one
like him.

The Blood of the Lamb exalted on
high magnified the greatest sacrifice
who paid thee ultimate price that we no
longer live our lives but to live our life
through him, life like him life and light
is him. The darkness is reveled the
lies are not conceled the truth
lives. pursuing life to give to thy
neighbor and thy brother loving
one another as God loved us. For
he gave His Son that we not
go on pursuing and craving sin
yet that we hunger and thirst
after God's righteousness. there's
no reason to believe that He
can't keep you and me. He is perfect
in power and in wisdom and
we are to be found in Him.

The Blood of the Lamb our identity
is soley in he blameless without
fault, striving running and chaseing
after perfection we are the selection
marked by grace abiding not in
deception consuming infections the sin
that causes you or me not to be
God's reflection. His image is the picture
of our living. Who dares to say or cares
to say how is it done? Allow the
only begotton Son the only Perfect
One nothing and no one under the sun
can teach us as the Holy One. How
to live, How to give, more and more of
ourselves. Forsaking our wants
allowing God to provide our needs, this is
the season that we remain on our
knees in prayer singing hymns and
meditating on the Lord decrees.
In Christ is eternal life and he
has given us the keys.

Lead Me Home

My sins have overtaken me; my enemies
have trampled over me. I know that you're
the One and only, who has the power to defeat
my enemies. I have sold my body for money,
I have destroyed my temple my love for self
has crimpled, Lord I can't see my vision is
blurry. All I have is song hymns and prayers
and I'm holding on even though I feel like
my prayer is not reaching your ears. I have
murdered my brother, I have caused my
family to suffer, and right now my
heart is troubled lead me home.

Sexual immorality is all I know, it gets
me closer than close. Each man makes
me feel like a woman even some make
me feel lower than low, it makes up for
being lonely and helps my pockets grow.
My mom is strung out on drugs, my brothers
never showed me love but, granny always
taught me that you're nothing but love. You
are the one I should put no one above.
There's a little voice screaming for help,
there are people who abused me not thinking
twice about how I felt. Living in a fantasy is
the closes to reality; I'm drugged up on
material things, being a prostitute gives me
fortune and fame. Yet, am I lost yet have
I broken your laws. All that I have

done has caught up to me and has
left a scar and from you I feel
So far. Lead me home

I need you now, I'm ready to take my
life as I think about the lives I took, the
devil hands that I shook. You have
provided me with salvation so I
repent now Lord Show me how. Not
because of my grief, because I know deep
down inside this is not me. Living a life
that's unpleasing to you doing the very
things you told me not to do! You are
nothing but truth! Eternal and everlasting
my enemies are laughing I have a gun to
my head and I feel like blasting it. Lead
me home. You are the best thing that ever
happen to me I repent Lord
please forgive me Lord, and Lead me home.

How He Loves Us

Oh, How He Loves Us, to be hung
On a cross spite the current condition
Of our hearts! Wicked, lost and needs
CPR, Christ prepared righteousness.
The bliss to love others how he loves
Us He paid the cost that we deserve
And the fact of how some of us go on,
Walking around like His blood shed for
Our sins mean nothing. To go on repeating
The same sin when the fact is He died for
Our sins! Yes the same ones you go on
Repeating again and again.

Oh, How He Loves Us. His arms
Are open and has been even before
The beginning of our existing. A God
Who we call Abba who has no
Beginning and no ending to His
Existence yet He gives us the privilege
Through Jesus Christ to know the hope
Of eternal life. One question lay…
When will you get it right, allowing
Jesus to perfect your Life! Crucifying
your flesh to the point that it dies
and in Christ be made alive.
Oh, How He Loves Us.

Apostasy

Apostasy caused by satan and
produces no good fruit but false
prophesies. God determines who's
justified by their faith. In this line
God is calling the unbelievers to
believe. For far too long you have
been deceived the very thing the
bible tells us to be careful of, trusting
the wrong breed of people enticing
devils evil doers and malicious
creatures.

Apostasy comes from
not being able to recognize the
tree that bares bad fruits their
cursed from their roots. Turn away
from their lies and be introduced
to the truth. Cursed is the man
who sow bad seeds knowingly
intentionally use others to deceive.
The time is now to know Christ and
believe all that he have in store for
those that believe! Ears have not
heard and eyes have not seen.

Apostasy, The time is now to
stand against the wickedness
of this world, that's deceiving

little boys and little girls. Adults,
leading their very own children
down the wrong road. Making
each child vulnerable, teaching them
to lie and steal because you do it
yourselves. this is how you live,
and you think they're not watching?
Keep doubting...Then you parents
can't sleep at night when they begin
to live a reckless life not thinking
twice. The way you live
do not lead them right.

Apostasy,
you fell away from the truth or renounced
your faith in Christ. The One who
gave you life. Influential false
teachers collecting their people may
the blood of Jesus cancel the plans
of these false teachers. This insults
a true believer. Professed believers
may fall away because of persecution
or love of the worldly things.

Allow
the Lord to examine your hearts
repent don't flinch the Holy Spirit
was sent. Apostasy will not come
if believers stay grounded in the
truth. Ask yourself have Apostasy
embraced you? Come back now!
that devil is a fool satan the Lord

God rebuke you. My brothers and
sisters are turning from your ways
today not by what they see but by
their faith. Satan you and your back
riding demons today we have
renounced your name.

Kill, Steal and Destroy

Growing up as a child, realizing life is full
of surprises. What was made of truth was
imitated and hidden in a veil degrading
the truth. Authorities conveying lies to be
reality, the truth is the Adversary attempt to
prevent our faith. Yet, extend brutality,
promote peace, but arrange calamity.
Open up your eyes to the light, darkness is
not friends to a believer they constantly
fight! Society trapped by the furs and feathers,
the worst is yet to come and the portray is…
it's going to get better. What do you
rather? the wisdom of a fool or the truth?
You choose. It's very simple open up
your hearts to Christ and you will know
the truth.

Many times were deceived refuse the truth
to afraid of a tree that is recognized by its
fruits. The limbs are shady and have damaged
roots. Their impersonal is not so personal.
You're exposed by the Holy Spirit you deny
Christ but serve kernel. Military respect,
spiritually deselect separate your opinions
from the facts. Christ came to save us
from captivity He is our liability. No longer
depending of self but the trinity. Check out
your faith it's descending around the wrong
crowd instead of you moving them you're
trending in the wrong direction, time for a

reflection who's your selection? The devil
deception or Christ perfection. My sins does
not have dominion over me, man does not
have opinion over me. I am Christ breathed
I'm not concerned with the tricks under
your sleeves, souls need to be saved
and unbelievers need to believe,
Christ came to save you and me.

One Life to Live

I can see, that you're to involve with your
fleshly life. Your roads are dark, and there
is not one street with light. Consumed,
with what you an only see. Stripped, from
all things spiritually. "Man I got one Life to
live" is what you say out loud! What if, you
were tossed in the lake of fire to be burned
for eternity, because of your sin? Then you
wouldn't make that statement so proud.

You're too afraid to be who God called you
to be, more concerned about your name in
the streets. God made the heavens and
the earth. Kids dying innocent blood tell me…
What is your street life worth? Money, power,
and respect? So that God's word can be
neglect… You're living your life out of a
dangerous fantasy, wake up to reality. Kill off
your hatred that's creating brutality. You're
looking at life from a small peep hole.
The dynamics of you living your life so
closed minded be reminded your living your
life trying to suit this world in and out of the
clubs rejecting God's love.

Then you go on denying not mentioning
you're not preparing for Christ arriving…
Every year you have a new year's

resolution, not being effective in the solution. It's your spirit that you're polluting with the idol things that you're choosing. So in the end, you tell me who's loosing. You have one life to live, so you live it like a heathen, your next breath is not guaranteed to be breathing! Who do you believe in? How long will you go on not believing? You're adding to the cross and the Holy Spirit is grieving. Come, come now and experience remission caused by your repentance.

Influenced by satan

satan has stepped in your life, turned you
left when the Lord our God told you right.
He has buried his presence in your life; he
has imparted strife in your life. Hear the
Spirit of God. You that have ears your
actions have made you ill, you are sick
spiritually, mentally and literally. To you,
you say satan did this and satan did
that. But, guess what? You are so
influenced by satan he don't have to
control you.

He has you, in fact he is not worried
about you, see he is laughing
at your sin and nakedness. Like a bad
seed planted will flourish on its own
like once you're so influenced by wrong,
it becomes your life! You have turned
from my knowledge and is cut off from
my glory... here is a parable satan went
to Jesus and tempted Him and Jesus told
him to flee. But you sinful nation has invited
him in! He doesn't have to do anything
because his demons use you to dwell within.
Stop calling on satan when his ways has
manifested in you! You are so influenced
by satan he doesn't have to control you.

You call Lord, Lord, save me, keep me,
the truth is you don't want to be saved and

you don't want to be kept! I have given to you
and also give you now the time to repent.
I am far from you and making my presence
known to warn you. You are so influenced by
satan he doesn't have to control you.

You are a harlot for satan and famous to
the world, yet you are cut off from my
glory you are living a life that's not pleasing
to me. I'm not on your heart to seek; you
seek the things of this world. I'm on my throne
yet my eye's roam the earth and I know your
worth. Potentially it's me that you hurt; more
than anything you have destroyed your life.
The life that I have given you! Right now,
not tomorrow it's time to come to repentance.

Repent from your ways so that your soul
will be saved. Living of this world will never
fill you. You don't get enough and it's the
idol things you turn to. I sit high and look
very low I know the things that you think
I don't know. What you hide from man
is plain to me. I am the One of all, and your
ways I see. You are so focused on your natural
body! Don't you know that I have the power
to make your crooked straight, to turn away
from you and leave satan to have you? You
are so influenced by satan he don't have to
control you.

You are simply stuck in your ways, and refusing
to be saved. Yet, let me remind you! The
Heavens and earth I made, and I theLord
your God has the last say.

Our Fathers Love

"For God loved the world so much
that he gave his one and only Son,
so that everyone who believes in him
will not perish but have eternal life.
God sent his Son into the world not
to judge the world, but to save
the world through him.

"There is no judgment against
anyone who believes in him.
But anyone who does not believe
in him has already been judged for
not believing in God's one and
only Son. And the judgment is
based on this fact: God's light
came into the world, but people
loved the darkness more than the
light, for their actions were evil.
All who do evil hate the light and
refuse to go near it for fear their sins
will be exposed. But those who do
what is right come to the light so
others can see that they are doing
what God wants. (**John 3:16-21**) **NLT**

Examine Me

Examine Me Lord, Enter my heart and
penetrate my thoughts through Christ Jesus
my, our, sins were bought while we were still
in sin your love was great Unconditionally
and sweet to taste.

I pray examine me Lord, anything that's
in me that's not like you its time for it to go
late night creeps laying with men going to
sleep your looking down and hurting, this
life is not close to holiness.

Your plans for me are great I took this
life you gave me and turned it up side
down. Doing me in the clubs hanging out
all night, drinking and sniffing cocaine
Lord God examine me. These demons are
big and I know that you are bigger! This
gun is to my head and I'm ready to blast
this trigger. Your love is greater your
actions of favor examine me clean me
create in me a new me.

I close this door to the things that displeases
you. Train me in your ways, in spite of the
tragic I experianced in the building called
church. In spite of my pain and in spite of my
hurt. What's real is, I'm on my knees sending
petitions, appeals, and pleads create in me
a new me.

No longer do I desire to live according to me,
I tried my way and I couldn't trust myself.
Lust, greed and fornication took my breath.

Sin and guilt in my head my sin cut me off
from you and inside I am dead spiritually,
mentally and emotionally hear me Lord
suddenly this life flashed before me.

A whisper in my ear says this is not what
you have for me! Create in me a new me,
cleanse me examine me friends aka demons
are cool with me because I look just like them.
Pursuing sex, lies and greed the same thing that
cuts you from me and me from you! What
a great love I have abused I'm the fool. The
joke is on me, I take this time to speak I'm
coming out of these streets. Out of these clubs
that shows me no love yet, entice me, priced me,
to fail likely like he that oppose Thee. He is greater,
he's the Almighty! I stand to fight the adversary
not with carnel weapons Lord I know you got me.

Victory speak, how does that sound? The words
are sweet satan you are a liar I scream! You
had me gone, to the Lord I belong! Examine me
Lord I'm ducing this world poof be gone
to Jesus I belong.

No Greater Love

One thing I heard, and two
Things I understood! Our God
Alone is good! Faithful and true.
In fact, he never left you.

He carried us, his footprints in the
Quick sand our God alone created the
Heavens, this world, this very land in
which we stand. Untouchable and
unharmedfully equipped! Yes, we are
armed.

With the intentions to lead, this is
God's anointed breed. With the intentions
to inspire God is calling his people to seek him
higher and higher. With the intentions to
Follow Christ to all with sorrow there
Is some light, to all with sorrow
there is a light and everything
will be alright just seek God and
Follow Christ.

Will, desire, seeking God's Will means
Looking for what God wants to be
done, done, done and complete Not
incomplete come out of retreat and get
it done, Get it done let God's will be done.
He is priority he is number One. Second to
None! Before one is zero which is none

None could have done the great
Works of our Holy One.

Who waits? Who can stand to hear
the seventh cup, the voice from the
Throne claiming it is done, it is done
He is the Great I AM equal to none!

All false gods came after the fact, after
The fact that the Heavens and the
earth were created I am elated. I
Serve a true and living God, a God
who sent his son to change my ways
and his spirit to dwell in my heart.

Lord God, search my heart examine every
Part, pursue, pursue, pursue to follow
To overtake, to chase, to seek to yearn,
Yearn, yearn to be whole in everything
We do Lord God in everything we do
It shall be approved and pleasing
unto you.

Sow, Sow, Sow into this season, sow for
This reason that our reward is in Heaven
and it's God's blessings that were reaping.
Sow holiness, sow righteousness, Sow love
and kindness. Do it willingly, do it freely Lord
it's all about you and not about me, Increase,
Increase, Increase implement your ways in
me speak your word throughMe that souls
will be saved, not tomorrow But, today.
Your anointance, thee anointance makes
a difference in my life, my life the life that
you gave me you are the reason why I

believe not because of experience, but
because of into man you breathe you took
his rib, and created me.

Gravity, importance, significance of oneness
No more religion I choose relationship!
Father here I am take my ways and strip,
take my ways and strip, take my ways and
Strip no more resources but I know the
source. No more resources but we should
know the source! Lord here I am take your spirit
and pour. Lord, your power, your atmosphere,
and your force. Why? Why divorce? Why
separate from a love that's so great? A love
that's so great that you don't have to wait to
see His ways to communicate to your heart
that it's okay, that it's okay to love that it's
okay to place no one above. Thereis no
greater love there is no greater love.

Remnant

For out of Jerusalem will come a
Remnant, and out of mount Zion
a band of survivors the zeal of the
Lord Almighty will accomplish this.

Switched focus, switched
Entertainment, and switched my bliss.
God will get his glory even if the life
God gave me has to be at risk.

Time to survive believers let's ride.
Meaningless things have been set aside.
Meaningless things were set here so
that mankind can be trained to
Worship idol things, the very things
That pulls us further and further
Away from Our King.

Politically dumb, spiritually daft.
Earthquakes, tornados and
Famines the very things that were
Predicted truth is truth not contradicted…
America hasn't seen God's Wrath.

My Father I will obey, walking only
By faith, Health plans, economic
trouble. To those who are not strong will
Sway, trust in the Lord
To Him, pray. Believe this he with
little faith.

No time to waste no time
To delay. The church has been
Distorted how unfortunate,
Are presidents is a Christian
Yet, he's all for gay marriages and
Abortions, the Kingdom of God
You will not see. Turn from
Your wicked ways that you may live
Life for eternality.

God is the same today, yesterday
And forever more. The Word of God
does not change for man. We are His
People and is commanded to carry
Out his plans. Out of all this came
God's loyal survivors waiting for
His arrival. His word declares the signs
Of the times and you are still in denial.

Lead Me Home

My sins have overtaken me; my enemies
have trampled over me. I know that you're
the One and only, who has the power to defeat
my enemies. I have sold my body for money,
I have destroyed my temple my love for self
has crimpled, Lord I can't see my vision is
blurry. All I have is song hymns and prayers
and I'm holding on even though I feel like
my prayers are not reaching your ears. I have
murdered my brother, I have caused my
family to suffer, and right now my
heart is troubled lead me home.

Sexual immorality is all I know, it gets
me closer than close. Each man makes
me feel like a woman even some make
me feel lower than low, it makes up for
being lonely and helps my pockets grow.
My mom is strung out on drugs, my brothers
never showed me love but, granny always
taught me that you're nothing but love. You
are the one I should put no one above.

There's a little voice screaming for help,
there are people who abused me not thinking
twice about how I felt. Living in a fantasy is
the closes to reality; I'm drugged up on
material things, being a prostitute gives me
fortune and fame. Yet, am I lost yet have
I broken your laws. All that I have

done has caught up to me and has
left a scar and from you I feel
So far. Lead me home

I need you now, I'm ready to take my
life as I think about the lives I took, the
devil hands that I shook. You have
provided me with salvation so I
repent now Lord Show me how. Not
because of my grief, because I know deep
down inside this is not me. Living a life
that's unpleasing to you doing the very
things you told me not to do! You are
nothing but truth! Eternal and everlasting
my enemies are laughing I have a gun to
my head and I feel like blasting it. Lead
me home. You are the best thing that ever
happen to me I repent Lord please forgive
me Lord, and me Lead me home.

Out-Pouring Poems

Out-Pouring Poems

I die to me, to live for you
I found a Love
Change of Heart
I don't know what you came to do
Let your Light Shine
I Love Him
Yes

I die to me, to live for You

I made up in my mind that I will create
a new change in me. Resisting the
devil, accepting Jesus and dying to me.

Do you believe Jesus died for you and me?
I'm talking about Jesus Christ you see!
His blood was shed so that you can no
longer live in the flesh getting knocked up,
committing adultery, and fornication
sexual immorality using sex in ways
that's not pleasing to God.

I glorify Christ, he delivered me. So, I die to
me to live for you. Who am I based on my
History? I'm God's chosen vessel and no longer
living in a mystery. He showed me his love
through his grace and mercy. I thank
God for his salvation, based on the
exercising of my faith.

I'm not perfect and can never be. Yet I will
strive for perfection as long as I breathe.
See, I been in this world and I gave it up
and learning everyday. Learning to submit
my life to Christ and not the world
opinionated belief. Not talking this
life but walking it in Christ light no more
satan will I live for you saying
I love God but caking you.

See, I been in this world and I've been
your fool. I gave you up when I
accepted Jesus Christ as my Lord
and savior this time around I repented
and understood the purpose of our savior.

Ask yourself who do you favor? Jesus
Christ or the familiar spirits speaking
in your ear telling you to do what's
contrary to the Holy Spirit. Line your
life up with what you say you're about
because where there's perfect love
there is no doubt.

Sinful natures are from satan, defile spirits
what are you creating? No longer living for
this world or me. Jesus is the head of my life,
directing my thoughts, my decisions ordering
my steps and yes I can take constructive
criticism.

I walk in meekness, patience and
strength under control so in the end
cast down your sins that lies deep
within. Come correct again. Live for
Christ abandon the perpetual entice
of satan, Glory to God, I die to me
to live for you.

No longer living a lie
but walking in truth. The voice is
stern yet; my heart yearns
righteousness, holiness, boldness, No
longer holding back what's within.

This is me, so my question is do
you still accept this person called me?
Wake up and realize Christ is not a
game. He died so that your sins
can no longer remain. Yet, you are bopping
to your worldly music constantly refusing
to give up the cares of this world so that
you can kick it with your homeboys or
your homegirls. Ungodly conversations
your daily deliberations cussing you're
constantly constipating rather you want
to live for God or for satan.

Wake up, I die to me so that Christ can increase
how much longer do you want to
live in retreat? Stop running away from
your sins confront them and tell them
no longer can they live within.

How many more times do you want God to
forgive you? You know what you're
doing yet you still do what you do.
Manipulating the truth convincing
yourself it will be okay if I …. work
this sin again, like have sex with this
man or woman without marriage a
vow made before God in heaven
or fulfill my worldly desires and forsake
his commandments now look at me
living subject to me saying I love Jesus
yet I can't give up my worldly deeds.

Now let me enlighten you on this.
What's impossible to man is possible
with God. Peter said to Jesus

(We left all we had to follow you).
Jesus replied I tell you the truth no
man has left home, wife, brothers,
parents, or children for the Kingdom
of God will fail to receive many times
as much in this age and the age to come
eternal life.

Only what you do for Christ
will last. Did you hear me say a sinful
nature is not from Christ? He died
just so we can be forgiven his
blood was shed just so we don't sin
that sin again. Repentance. Don't look
at me but hear the Spirit of the Lord
Through me he who has an ear let
him hear what the Spirit of the Lord has
to say. I heard what the Spirit of the
Lord said to me and it pierced my soul.
Jesus said. I know your deeds that
you are neither cold or hot so because
you are lukewarm neither hot or cold
I am about to spit you out of my mouth.
There's no in between with God, Choose
ye this day who you will serve.
Without holiness no one will see the Lord.

I want no credit but to glorify his name,
I die to this flesh so Christ can live
and dwell in me. So that I can help
someone else who is in need, and they
too will see just by my walk and not my
talk. I live it, I'm learning, I'm grasping
I study to show myself approve rightly
dividing the Word of Truth. I die to me

no more satan away from me.
With your imitating beliefs.

Rest assured I'm mailing you back your
worldly gifts Fed Ex packaged you
will receive it in Same Day Delivery stamped
Child of God I must say you had me
gone thinking sex, lies, lust and ungodliness
wasn't wrong. So listen, I'm on my way to
take back my brothers and sisters from
you! Lost souls, hungry children, opening
up trash bags to find thrown away infants.
Youth confused don't know if they want to
be a man or a woman (Those are spirits).
And it didn't start here study on Sodom
and Gomorrah. Who will attempt to
stop it? Naked women in the clubs selling
their souls their temples are unclean
therefore their bodies are infected.
Who's going to help correct it? See
when you're living for God these things
hurt you to see. All you should want to do
is change the world starting with the change
in you through Jesus Christ. God Will be
done, a new heaven and a new earth
Seek ye first! Understand that Christ must live
in you that his work may be complete in you.
Be true to He that is truth. Help others
to believe the truth that Jesus is the only way
to God. You were on a high from this world but
I stand to tell you, you haven't
experienced the natural high that
comes from the Most High. So again,
attention I'm coming to take
my brothers and sisters. God

will use me so be careful because your
schemes, tricks, lies, deception, and your
ungodliness have now been rejected.
Father I die to me, to live for you.

I Found a Love

I found a love that does not fail.
A love that prevails despite myself,
I found a love that's beyond measures
Of deserving. Yet, have I opened my
Heart to receive! yet has my faith
Been increased to believe!

A Love that's rare a love that's not fit to
Compare. Love was always there!
To ponder on the days that we
Live in; men are lovers of
Themselves rejecting a love that's
Rare a love that's not fit to compare.
Men are lovers of themselves building
Their foundation on what they have
Defined by material things they
Incline in this rejecting he that is divine
He that is prime, He that is prime!

I found a love that is primary of my
Life, oh generation put away your
Jealousy and strife. Allow Jesus to
Be Lord over your life! Seek, search
And you will find.

See this has nothing to do with
Religion everything to do with he
That has risen, in him I am prisoned
Married to Him I am committed. Oh,
Generation become committed to

Our God.

Finding His love finding He that is
Love gives you peace through
Every storm. Causing you to go beyond
The four walls and sitting in the pews
Yet getting up going to work the
Harvest fulfilling the great commission
And doing the very thing God called
You to do.
Romans 8:30 says this; and those
Whom he predestined He also
Called and those who he called
He also justified and those whom
He justified he also glorified. In this,
Let's be the salt of the earth and
A light to the world, for I have found
A Love!

Change of Heart

I'm longing for the day when all
hearts will be changed, the literacy
of Spoken Word Poetry and the
encouragement that Christ is the
way. Dying to my sins as I repent
daily. I know it's bigger than you and
me, Christ purpose and presence on
earth saved me, so my brothers and
sisters who are victims of this world
lost hope, mothers and fathers on
dope leaving their children stranded
feeling like there is no hope.

There is a way out I'm not talking
about being locked down behind
prison doors nor am I talking
about killing one another creating
war. See, this is what Christ died for
so we can no longer live in the flesh
doing what we want putting one
another down instead of building
one another up seeing one another
dying literally and not offering to help.

I'm longing for the day when all
hearts will be changed. When we
will no longer be locked down
in prison chains. Let's open our heart
to Christ which will cause our thinking

to change and we will start using our
brain being led by the Spirit of God
using the Word of God to remain wise.
The things of this world is temporary to
the flesh and the time is now to take heed
to the Word of God and place our
treasures in Heaven.

Only what you do for Christ
will last and when you repent of
your sins God don't remember the
ones in the past, given you a clean
slate come to the alter please don't
wait. For thee alter is the place where you will
meet Christ. Open your heart and he will
meet you where you are.
Give your life to Christ, maybe
you did this before, let's do it twice.
Whatever it takes for you to get it right
with Christ. You don't have to be behind
The four walls of a church. Fall on your knees
Now and accept Jesus Christ in your life.
Open up your mind and heart to his teachings.
Make ready your heart that it be the place
Where God dwells.

I'm longing for the day when all hearts
will be changed. I'm not saying that
I have a dream but longing for the
day that all hearts will be changed.
I'm here to take part in fulfilling the
gospel. One of the very reasons
why Christ came so we can all be
exposed to the Good News and our
souls can be saved. Jesus knew that we were

Not fit to go to the cross so He went for
us, taking our sins with Him. No more
idol thinking creating the worst in
you, no more being manipulated
of your gifts and being fooled.
The time is now to have a purpose
driven life and soar despite the detours.
Time to live according to what the Most High
has destined for us. Stop living a lie
and be more effective in your will
to try and tell your flesh it's
time to die join me in changing lives.

I'm longing for the day when all hearts
will be changed. Many want to rep the
hoods because it's known for its violence,
wake up and realize how many young
ones are following. You're the very one
who makes being a g' or a thug seem
cool, gun play is what you say but in God's
eyes out of the wise man you're the fool.
You call carnal minded being true you're
lost brother take hint to the
context clues, Christ
came to save me and you.

I'm longing for the day when all hearts
will be changed. Just thinking about it
makes me weak, just thinking about it
makes me weep, so I just fall to my
knees and give Jehovah praise you see,
he's all that we need, he's all that you need.

I'm longing for the day when all hearts
will be changed. I'm longing for the

day when the churches will come back
to the Good News that God has
provided salvation for all people
through the atoning of Jesus
death stop teaching the people to
give all they have left financially
start teaching that if they don't get
it right they will burn for eternity.

Start teaching them to repent and
turn from their wicked ways so
that they soul will be saved. Their so many
saints in the congregation that's
spiritually dead and you are challenging their
giving and they haven't changed the way
their living but it's okay to you because
they are still giving and giving. What ever
happen to sacrifice, that all give up their
fleshly life and all pick up their cross and
follow Christ? The distortion ain't right and
each man is held accountable for that
which he know some leaders are to
afraid to see others grow so you
say your moving to fast, take it slow.
All the individual want to do is
be on fire for Christ and you tell them
be careful of their zeal because it
might not be right, Christ said bless
are those who hunger and thirst after
that which is right.

I'm longing for the day when all hearts
will be changed. It ain't time to make it
rain when Christ blood poured from the
crown of his head to the sole of his feet,

I'm telling you now Christ blood speaks.
There aint no need to walk it out if in
the back of your head you doubt that
Christ presence on earth
was to take our sins out.

I Don't Know What You Came to Do

I don't know what you came to do but,
I came to live for the Lord. To walk in
humility and carry my sword. To live
according to His holiness, to cast out
devils and reject worldly desires.
It's not in this world but, in God I receive
my reward. I don't know what you came
to receive but, in Jesus Christ I believe.
And by the way it's not man that approves
me. I was chosen and ordained before
my natural birth so I'm going to serve
where it hurts.

May your ears be attentive and hearts
be sensitive because, this Child of God
isn't playing church. On this rock Jesus
build His church. Nothing missing,
lacking or broken but, anointed and
ready for The Lord's down pouring.
There has been some distortion in the
hearts of many and where this poetry
came from there's plenty. I'm here to
be used for my spirit is willing.

Like really, these false indictments
isn't funny. To articulate the perpetrate
it doesn't take a scientist but, the discerning
of spirits. A spiritual gift which enables

certain believers to tell the difference
between true and false teachers.
I don't know what you came to do but,
I came to serve; to be used as a vessel
Through me the Spirit of God will be
heard. The ungodliness will be effectively
purged. Here I am Lord, examine my
heart. Use it, rule it, feel it, mold it, make it,
shape it, test it, hear it, dwell in it, have your
way in it. Your praise is in it, your glory is in it,
and your commands are tied to it. The fear
of you is in it, the belief of your Son is in it.

Hear this; I don't know what you came
to do but, I came to be humbled. See,
when it comes to the Lord our God
I will not stumble; over His word just to see
souls misled, just so that the offering tray
can be fed! Question, what's going
through your head?

See I studied the four gospels
and Jesus of Nazareth; I set the DVD
to repeat it played even when I was sleep.
Revelation has come to me. Each man
was healed by their faith to believe.
Jesus asked for each man to go and
sin no more, so what is this deception,
wickedness false teaching knocking at the
door?

Lord, this is a dying nation and a great
portion of the buildings called church is
spiritually rapping this generation. See I'm
here to stand up in their faces the Kingdom

of God is at hand and this church here, for it is
written the gates of hell can't prevail against it.
Powerfully, the word of God declares it.
I don't know what you came to do but,
I came to bear testimony not to detest
the phonies but make them aware that
Jesus Christ is the only way to God.

Through Christ, were made holy and set
apart. Take this warning and unhardened
your hearts. Stop looking for what makes
sense when the New Testament is a
supernatural covenant. Not implemented
for the natural but, you have made this a
hassle, because you open your mind and
close your hearts! In your minds theirs
delusions and satan has taken you for a
walk in the park birthing confusion. With his
Ways and his thoughts. But, God holy laws
you fought.

I don't know what you came to believe
but, I came to represent the truth to
recognize a tree by its fruits! I came to
pick up my cross and carry my sword,
and live according to God's holiness
completely representing the Kingdom
Of God! Amen

Let your Light Shine

From a young child she was envied
and maliciousley decieved. Family
friends you name it! They had all
concieved a passion to destroy what
they had seen in her. At that time
she didn't even see it in herself.
Day after day living her life with jelousey
spirits around her camp wondering and
praying to God when will he turn off her lamp.

Everywhere she went her light
shined. Not outdoing but, outgrowing
this world to live a life for Christ. High looks
on her, because everyone thought she
was so perfect little did they know all
she wanted was to be accepted and turn
her light so that whoever was around her, their
light will shine.

She believed in truth but recieved
so many lies from all who claimed
they love her. The Holy Spirit showed
her their intentions and motives to despise
her. Can you believe she lived her life in a
corner. Feeling rejected, neglected and
misunderstood by everyone except
her Father in heaven. That caused her
to seek God harder crave him deeper
in the mean time her relationship

with God grew stronger.

From young no one understood
her, so all they could do is say they were
with her, yet they were so against her.
Who can she love? Who can
she trust? When this world is consumed
with images false witnesses envy strife
jealousy abiding in her premisses.
God taught her. Humbleness, meekness
and patience will work out perserverance
for the elevation in her life.

In order for her to succeed in her
walk with God... She understood
that if they hated her, they hated
the Son first and no longer was
she the victim but, the victor. My
story, her story is a blessing
and not a curse. I could have, would
have, should have striked back
when my sister set me up for destruction.
When i was persecuted, lied
on talked about... rapped of my gifts
but not of my purpose. I could have
striked back, But I stood on the
promises of God.

The Lord said in his word that he
will grant the enemies who rise up
against me to be defeated before
me they will come at me from one
direction and flee in seven. Silent No
More I open my mouth to speak that
living in that corner has run its course

and if the enemy doesn't like it...
he has no choice he can get
on board to only be thrown off!
Because, I will be who God
called me to be. No more will I
turn my light off so that others can
shine. I will encourage you stand up
and be who God called you to be,
becuase he lives in you just
like he lives in me.

I Love Him

I Love him like, if no one was
around as long as his presence
was there. It's like a love that's
rare because, I tried the Love
of family and friends and it is so
flaw because they love with only
half of their heart leaving the other
half available for compromise.
I love him, because, with him I can
be myself and where correction is
needed he will make me aware.
Despite what I've done and where I
been He has taken me in and opend his
hands. Like even when I was doing wrong
he was right there to convict me. He is
the reason I thought twice he is the
reason I thought man this just not right.

I Love him, Like the Father
I never had whenever I was
disappointed emotionally hurt
or even as a child being sad I
will envision running to him and
rap my arms around his neck
and cry on his shoulder he
was the only one there.

I Love him, he has always been there.
He knew I can only take so much so
whenever I was ready to throw

in the towel to my rescue he would be,
my rampart and strong tower. I love him,
an unfailing love! Until you experienced
his love only then will you know
how to truly love.

I Love him, he's one
person I don't want to disappoint,
hurt, deny, reject, fight, betray
or delay when I can serve him today.
I love him, he has always wanted
the best for me never lying nor leading
me down the wrong path, if I
took the wrong path that led to
destruction it was because of me
and guest what? He still saved me.
Only by his; love, grace and mercy.

I Love him, like I sacrifice all that
I am or want to be so that he
can mold and make me and form me
into everything he intended me to be.
See this is the Love I'm talking about a
love you don't have to question or
doubt the Love that makes you want to
shout. I Love him like with no limits
I bow down and worship him. I trust
him so much I don't have to question
him. All that he has done has turn
out for my good he taught me how
to understand when at the time it
wasn't meant to be understood.

I Love him, he taught me the things
he reveal to me are supernatural and

not designed to make sense to the
natural. My Lord, God, Jesus Christ
thank you for being up with me in
the middle of the night I know that you
don't slumber nor sleep I Love you
and thank you for listening to me.
Thank you, I yield to you whatever you
want me to do I was created to please
you and glorify you and give you
praise for the rest of my days you're
the only Father I have ever known
you taught me that I will reap what
I have sown and how to accept it
because it was my sinful
natures that created it.

I love you, and to me you mean more
than Eternal Life I give you the life that
you gave me and for the rest of my
days I give up my worldly ways because,
I truly, unconditionally, sincerely unlimitedly
ultimately unsurprisingly faithfully
radically effectively willingly Love you.

Yes

Yes to your will, and yes to your way. For
this I'm going all the way. Lord it
was your grace, your mercy you heard
me, you loved me you comforted me
you kept me and you showed me. You
allowed me to face hypocrisy you
saved me you said yes to me. Yes, so
blessed not stressed, and my life is not a mess.
Despite my ways you have seen my best. Yes,
what do you require of me, great is
your purpose for me, what do you expect
of me, what do you need from me, it's
not about me but all that I was
ordained to be. Yes, you are my
Father, you are my brother, you are
my sister, you are my mother, you
are like none other and
for me your Son suffered.

Yes, more of you, all of you I trust you;
I need you I crave you I rest in you
I find peace in you. This is so real this
is beyond man. See I feel your
presence even when I'm sleep.
when I don't feel your presences
I weep. See, you waited patiently
for me. And eventually I said
yes to you and I said yes to me.
Yes, You Fathered me biologically
you taught me, you trained me, and you

stood up for me. You helped me,
you believed in me you guided me,
and you placed your Will in me, and you
expect more and more of me. Yes,
I chose You I live for You I desire
You I'm inspired by You I adore You
I cherish You I appreciate You I love
You, I worship You
I praise You I give up all for You.

Yes, tell me what you really need
show me where you want me to be.
Yes, I don't want you for just a
season I want you for every reason
I want you every hour, minute,
second, and split second of the
day from now even in my old age.
I want you for my vengeance
I want you to remove all of my
hindrance I want you to do all that
you have intended. I need you more
then periodically you are the reason
why I believe, not because of man you
get all the glory. Yes, you stripped me
you disciplined me you showed me
how to seek you only. Yes, I run to
You, I cry to You I can't lie to You
I'm real with You; I put no one above
You. Yes, yes to your will and yes
to your way and this I'm taking
to my grave. To me you said yes.
To You I give exceedingly
beyond my best YES.

Prayer's and Hymns

Show up
Comfort Me
Endurance
Through You
You're First
Encamp Me

Show Up

Lord, your servant
Heart is heavy. According to your
Promise show up! I have prayed
Longing for you to save me out of
This distress I have kept your precepts
I have loved and prayed for my enemies.
Lord, creator of heavens and earth you
Made me and know all about me show up.
Selah,

Comfort Me

Comfort me Lord like a child without
A father I need you! My first and last
Father, you are the only Father I know
Like a Father to his daughter you're my comfort.
You're anointing, sweet anointing. Comfort me,
These storms have blown me in many areas yet
I find peace in you. Comfort me. I long to rest on
Your shoulder and weep in your arms, comfort me.
Selah,

Endurance

Lord above all things, I praise you
For what you have done, I worship
You for who you are. Your presence
Is my resting place. I dwell in your
Righteousness, I long to be in right
standing with you. I know that if I come
out of your presence there will be an internal
disaster, a spiritual wicked entrapment. This
Is the trick of the enemy that waits for me
The Lord God rebuke he. I lookTo thee my
Father the Almighty Have your way in me,
may your spirit lead and guide me
Exactly where YOU want me to be.

Selah,

Encamp Me

Encamp me, consume me, your fire, a
Burst of desire to be your vessel see this
I'm taking personal. Encamp me with your
Fear. Here am I, I'm right here on my knees
I bow to you with petitions encamp me with your
Truth. Encamp me now; stamp me now your child,
Your daughter in your presence your atmosphere
Heaven. Establish unrap it show your glory your Son,
Jesus! I'm your imitator ill be the undertaker your
Child a partaker. Out with the iniquity it will not
Control me! Encamp me. Your shelter, my helper
Creator works are greater your word is my shield
I wear it like a blazer, encamp me,
And surround me with your favor.
Selah,

Forgive Me

Lord forgive me for reaching a place
of dwelling in things that concerns me not,
My life is in your hands. Everything I need
Is in you. I will continue in the work that you have
Given me to do. I'm your vessel take me and use.
I know that you work all things work together for my good.
With gratitude I offer thanksgiving, for you are the
Source of my living. With so much going on
Around me, my giants surround me yet, I thank you
Unconditionally that your word grounds me.
Selah,

Through You

My Lord, I praise you for life through your Son
For he is the way that takes off my old man. After
Repentance of my sins I'm able to stand
As one holy to you, for my sins have been forgiven.
I come to you praying help me willingly I need thee to
Change the way I'm living. For, I cannot do this by myself
I come to you empty you're my help. Thank you, through you I
find Joy, Peace, Truth, and Love all that's divine. I find in you.
Selah,

Dominate Mission

Hear me when I say I'm on a mission
Not to sit around but to encourage the Lord's
vision, to embrace the lives of others. To revel who
I am in which all my life I tried to cover. Who
am I? I'm the mission that's here to serve
My purpose, to go beyond the expectations
of the enemy Curses.

He thought he had me Aha,
But, Jesus is my purpose. My mission,
My will to go on, to be strong to love
Spite of My tears, my fears and in spite
Of those who have persecuted me. I love you,
Youre apart of this mission too! Don't be perplexed
Of the fact that you don't have the victory
Over my tears, my fears more over
my Self-control.

Remember I'm on a mission,
Not to be stolen but, to be focus
And trust in the Salvation of God,
and not the failure provided
from man and delivered to me.
It's bigger then you, it's bigger
Then me. It's the dominate mission
That will bring trials
And tribulations of many kind.

Everyday I'm placed before my
Enemies, friends, and family

With a smile on my face,
But inside there's a sound crying out
To the Lord, Oh Lord hear me now.
Oh Lord hear me now.

What a beautiful thing it is to serve
My mission yet empower
the vision, with the Lord's divine
Permission. I've done my will thinking
I was taking the short cut to
Get to "my dreams". All the long my
dreams my desires was in
God's hands the best hands.
So I say, on this day. Every day,
And the rest of my days, I will to
Live for my Father in Heaven,
Representing the Kingdom of Heaven
In my mission.

Final Annotations

"Get up and prepare for action.
Go out and tell them everything I tell you to say.
Do not be afraid of them,
or I will make you look foolish in front of them.
For see, today I have made you strong
like a fortified city that cannot be captured,
like an iron pillar or a bronze wall.
You will stand against the whole land
the kings, officials, priests, and people of Judah.
They will fight you, but they will fail.
For I am with you, and I will take care of you.
I, the LORD, have spoken!" (**Jeremiah 1:17-19 NLT**)

Then I heard the voice of the Lord saying,
"Whom shall I send? And who will go for us?"
And I said, **"Here am I. Send me!"**
He said, "Go and tell this people:
"'Be ever hearing, but never understanding;
be ever seeing, but never perceiving.'
Make the heart of this people calloused;
Make their ears dull and close their eyes.
Otherwise they might see with their eyes,
hear with their ears, understand with their
Hearts, and turn and be healed." (**Isaiah 6:8-10 NIV**)

Jesus came and told his disciples, "I have
been given all authority in heaven and on
earth. Therefore, go and make disciples
of all the nations, baptizing them in the
name of the Father and the Son and the

Holy Spirit. Teach these new disciples to obey all the commands I have given you. And be sure of this: I am with you always, even to the end of the age."
(Matthew 28:18-20 NLT)